GUITAR CHORDS

FOR
BEGINNERS

EASY

GUITAR CHORDS

THAT SOUND AMAZING

GUITAR CHORDS
FOR BEGINNERS

ISBN-13: 978-1518720765

ISBN-10: 1518720765

Available in

all major bookstores

and online retailers worldwide

HomeGuitarAcademy.com

CONTENTS

HOW TO LEARN

Work on two chords at the time (*not one*). That way, you're speeding up the bit between the chords (chord changing) too. Whether you're a beginner or professional, D is D and G is G. But the professional is much faster between the two. And you will too...by learning two chords at a time.

3

SIMPLE STEPS

1 Tilt Your Guitar

2 Set Your Hand

3 Play The Chord

This Simple 3 Step Approach, combined with working on two chords at a time, dramatically increases the speed of your progress.

Open Chords - Tilt Back

1 - Tilt Your Guitar

Tilting makes guitar chords so much easier to play. The guitar is now doing some of the work for you.

It is also the key to fast chord changing, and making bar chords easier.

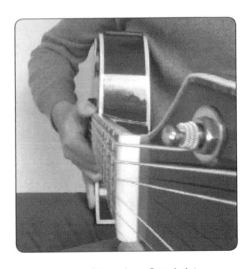

Bar Chords - Straight

2 - Set Your Hand

- Your fingers approach 3 ways
- Eliminates waste movement
- Makes playing chords easier
- Presets many chords that follow
- Guarantees good thumb positions

F Chord

Bar Chords

Open Chords

3 - Play The Chord

Learn the most important easy chords first - Easy Guitar Chords *(Page 13)* . Within days your fretting hand will be upskilled and ready for - The Most Played Guitar Chords.

To encourage you even more, ***Every Chord In This Book Is Technically Perfect***. And you can achieve in weeks, what took many people years to learn.

So Come on now....***Pick Up Your Guitar***...and start playing some amazing chords today.

Pauric Mather

DON'T DO THIS

There are *five reasons why people fail* to learn guitar chords. Avoid them and you have just about written your own guarantee of success. Here they are.

1. Weak fingers

2. Bad guitar teachers

3. Bad thumb positioning

4. Learning G the wrong way

5. Learning on nylon string guitars

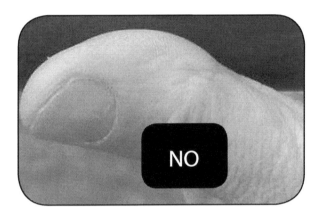

BAD THUMB

If your thumb is badly positioned, fast chord changing is impossible. Also your guitar will produce a muddy sound at the start of any chord you play.

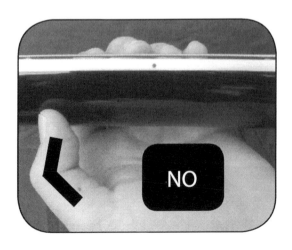

RAISED THUMB KNUCKLE

This locks your fingers. You might be able to learn some chords from this position....but you will never be able to change quickly from chord to chord.

TOO CROUCHED

Most beginners pull the guitar neck back and crouch out and down to see the strings.

Avoid this and you will learn and improve much much faster. And your guitar will be so much easier to play.

LEARNING G THE WRONG WAY

Learning G as shown here is one of the main reasons why people give up playing guitar.

This G only works when you pick each string one by one. But not when you strum all the strings at once. And it can lead to other problems as you try to improve.

YOUR GUITAR

Most professionals play slim necked - steel string - acoustic guitars. So should you. Once your fingertips harden they're much easier to play. They also sound much better than cheap nylon stringed guitars.

The neck width is also the same as an electric guitar. You'll be able to learn many skills needed for both instruments on one.

GIRLS

Many of you have smaller body frames than men so it makes more sense to learn on a smaller body sized and slim necked guitar.

As well as being much easier to learn on, and play, you'll be much more comfortable.

SLIM NECK

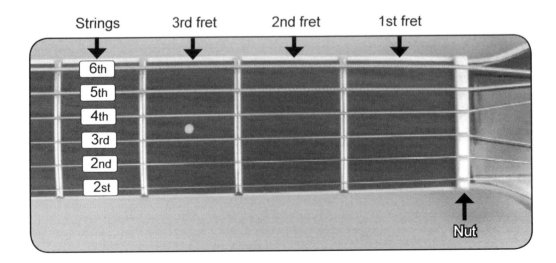

How you set up to play guitar has a huge impact on how quickly you learn. Can you **Sit Tall** and keep the **guitar neck angled out** *(about the length of your forearm).*

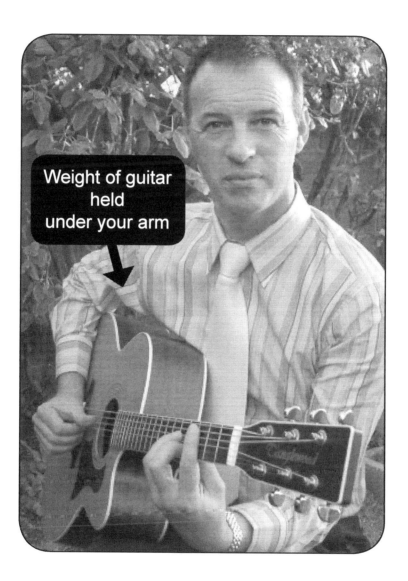

- Fretting hand in front of you

- Same position as turning a key

- Makes chord changing much easier

THE SECRET

Here is one of the great secrets of playing guitar. In fact without it nothing is possible. From The Eagles to Elvis and from California to New Zealand you'll see **"The Guitar Triangle"**.

This simple but life changing guitar tip helps people to accomplish in a few days, or even hours, what took many people years to achieve. It

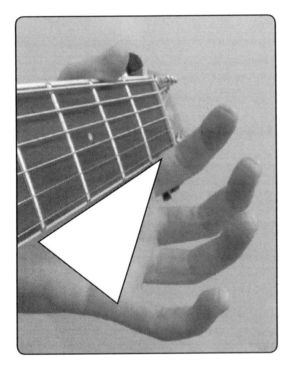

- Is in millions of songs

- Gives you a steady hand

- Releases your natural ability

- Keeps fingers in front of guitar

- Makes room for fingers to move

- Lets you play with your fingertips

- Lets your fingers play horizontal

- Keeps knuckles level / below fingers

- Prevents knuckles from collapsing

- Makes fingering much easier

- Makes chord changing much easier

If you watch any great guitarist in any style of music anywhere in the world you'll see - *The Guitar Triangle.*

> ### *Not In*
> Bar chords - Power chords - F chord

OPEN CHORDS

You can play thousands of songs without moving your
Thumb, 3rd finger, or Triangle.

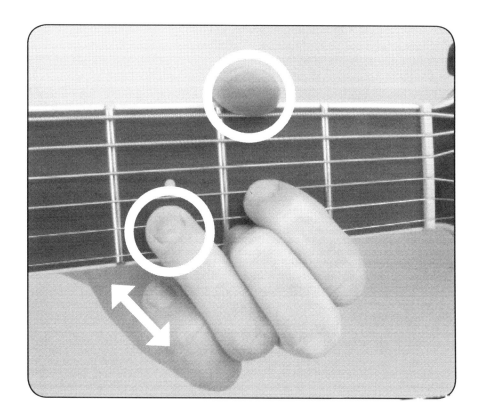

This simple technique keeps your fingers close to the fretboard. And because they have less distance to travel, your chord changing becomes much faster. It also eliminate all waste finger movement.

BAR CHORDS

1. Hold a mug in your fretting

2. Claw your hand and link 3rd & 4th fingers

3. Smae feeling as playing a bar chord

4. Holding your shape, take the mug away

5. Place your fingers on the fretboard

6. This is your hand position for bar chords

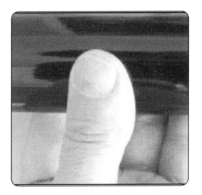

EASY
GUITAR
CHORDS

THAT SOUND AMAZING

A2

1

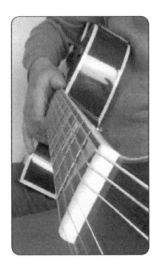

Page 4

FINGER	STRING	FRET
2nd	4th	2nd
3rd	3rd	2nd

2

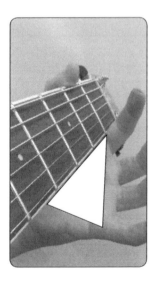

Page 10

3

- Thumb touches 6th stringt

Amaj7

1

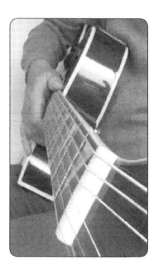

Page 4

2

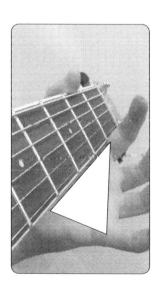

Page 10

FINGER	STRING	FRET
1st	2nd	5th
2nd	4th	6th
3rd	3rd	6th

3

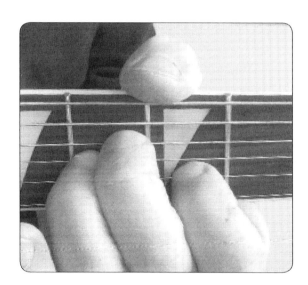

- Thumb touches 6th string
- 1st fingertip in corner of fret

Am7

1

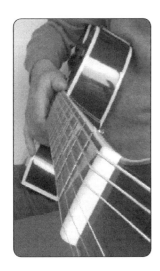

Page 4

2

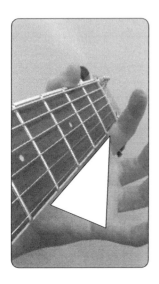

Page 10

FINGER	STRING	FRET
1st	2nd	1st
2nd	4th	2nd

3

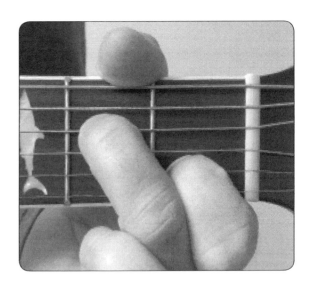

- Thumb touches 6th string
- 1st fingertip in corner of fret

A7

1

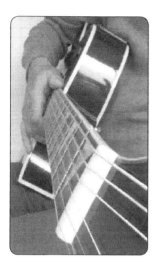

Page 4

2

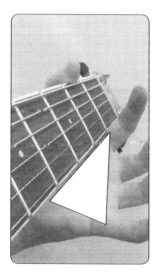

Page 10

FINGER	STRING	FRET
1st	4th	2nd
3rd	2nd	2nd

3

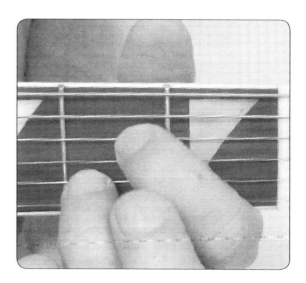

- Thumb touches 6th string
- 1st fingertip in corner of fret
- 3rd fingertip in middle of fret

A/E

1

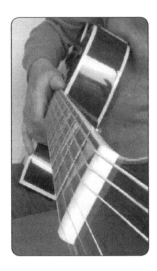

Page 4

2

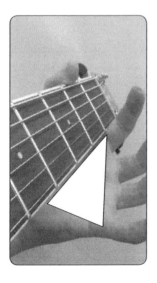

Page 10

FINGER	STRING	FRET
1st	3rd	6th
2nd	5th	7th
3rd	4th	7th

3

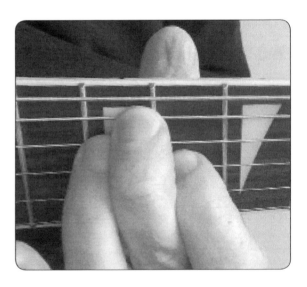

- Thumb can touch 6th string
- 1st fingertip in corner of fret

A add9

1

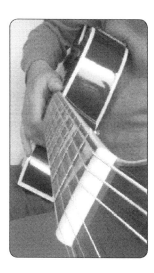

Page 4

2

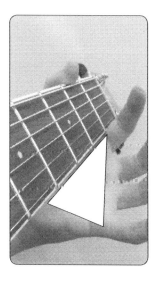

Page 10

FINGER	STRING	FRET
1st	3rd	2nd
2nd	5th	4th
3rd	4th	4th

3

- Thumb can touch 6th string
- 1st fingertip in corner of fret

Bm

1

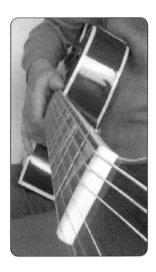

Page 4

2

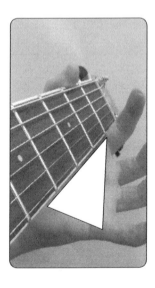

Page 10

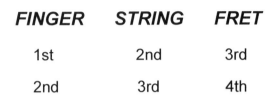

FINGER	STRING	FRET
1st	2nd	3rd
2nd	3rd	4th

3

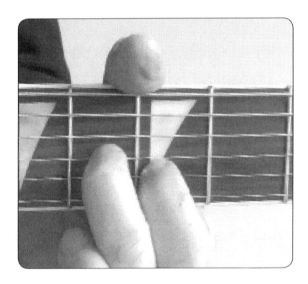

- 1st fingertip in corner of fret
- 2nd fingertip in middle of fret
- Strum bottom 4 strings

Bm sus4

1

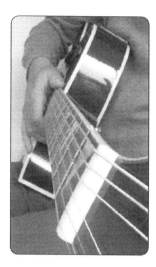

Page 4

2

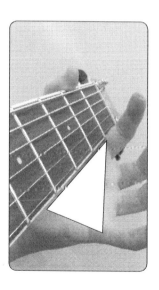

Page 10

FINGER	STRING	FRET
1st	2nd	3rd
2nd	4th	5th
3rd	3rd	5th

3

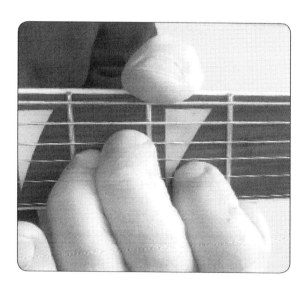

- Thumb can touch 6th string
- 1st fingertip in corner of fret

B/E

Often played instead of B

1

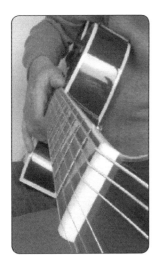

Page 4

2

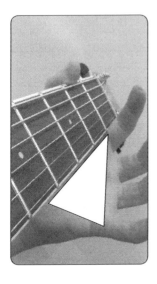

Page 10

FINGER	STRING	FRET
1st	3rd	8th
2nd	5th	9th
3rd	4th	9th

3

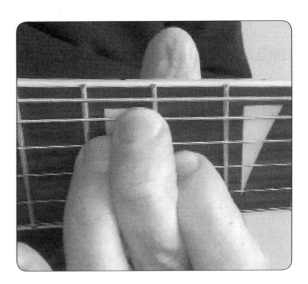

- Thumb can touch 6th string
- 1st fingertip in corner of fret

Cadd9

1

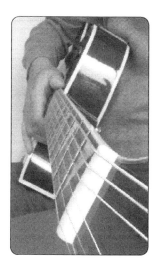

Page 4

2

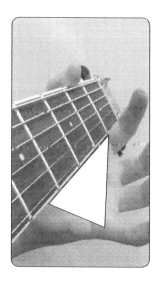

Page 10

FINGER	STRING	FRET
1st	4th	2nd
2nd	5th	3rd
3rd	2nd	3rd

3

- Thumb touches 6th string
- 1st fingertip in corner of fret
- 2nd & 3rd fingertips in middle of fret

Cmaj7

1

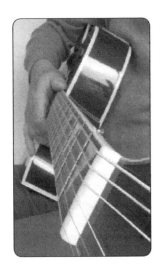

Page 4

2

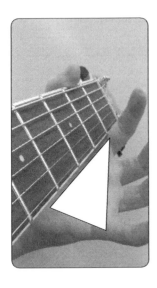

Page 10

FINGER	STRING	FRET
2nd	4th	2nd
3rd	5th	3rd

3

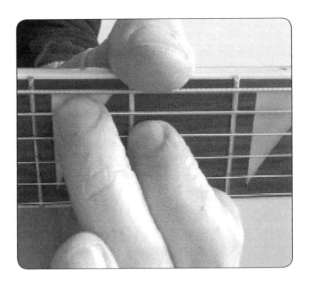

- Thumb touches 6th string
- 1st fingertip in corner of fret
- 2nd fingertip in middle of fret

C#m

Easy

1

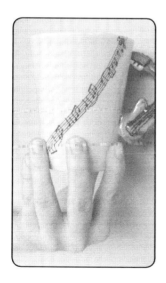

Page 4

2

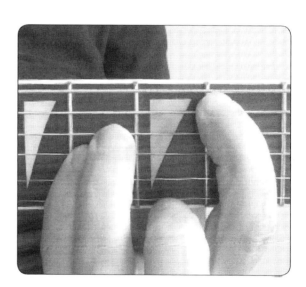

Page 12

FINGER	STRING	FRET
1st	5th	2nd
3rd	4th	4th
4th	3rd	4th

3

- 1st fingertip touches 6th string
- 2nd finger hovers over strings

D 7sus2

1

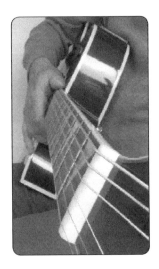

Page 4

FINGER	STRING	FRET
2nd	3rd	5th
3rd	2nd	5th

3

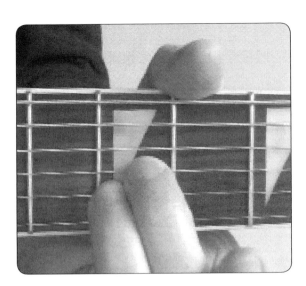

2

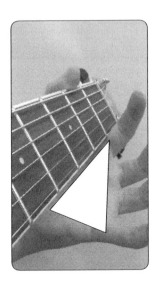

Page 10

- Thumb can touch 6th string
- Strum bottom 4 strings

D/E

1

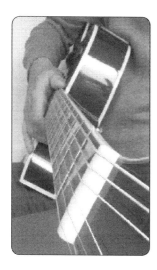

Page 4

2

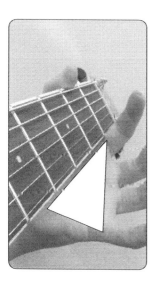

Page 10

FINGER	*STRING*	*FRET*
2nd	3rd	7th
3rd	2nd	7th

3

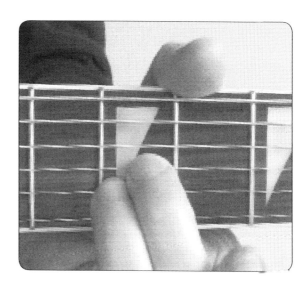

- Thumb can touch 6th string
- Strum bottom 4 strings

Dmaj7

1

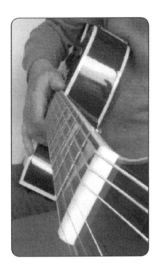

Page 4

2

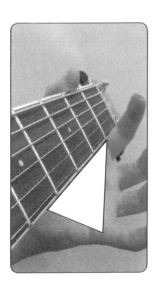

Page 10

FINGER	STRING	FRET
1st	1st	2nd
1st	2nd	2nd
1st	3rd	2nd

3

- Thumb touches 6th string
- 1st finger in corner of fret
- Strum bottom 4 strings only

Dmaj9

1

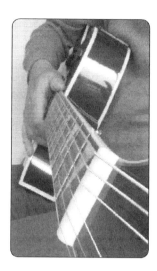

Page 4

2

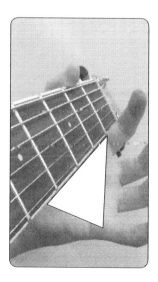

Page 10

FINGER	STRING	FRET
1st	3rd	2nd
2nd	2nd	2nd

3

- Thumb touches 6th string
- Strum bottom 4 strings only

D2

1

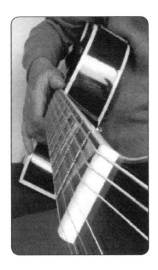

Page 4

FINGER	STRING	FRET
1st	3rd	2nd
3rd	2nd	3rd

3

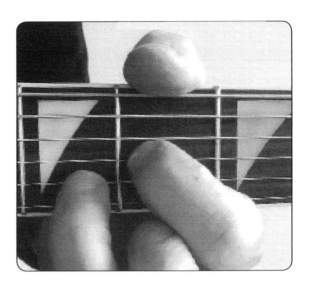

2

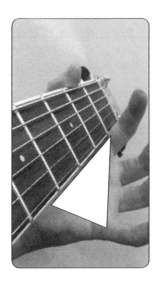

Page 10

- Strum bottom 4 strings only

D6

1

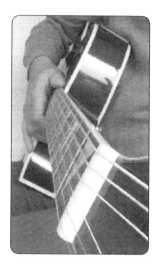

Page 4

2

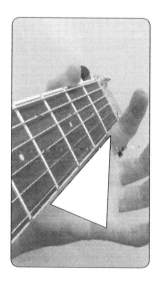

Page 10

FINGER	STRING	FRET
1st	3rd	2nd
2nd	1st	2nd

3

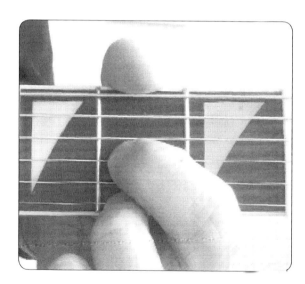

- Thumb touches 6th string
- Strum bottom 4 strings only

Em7

1

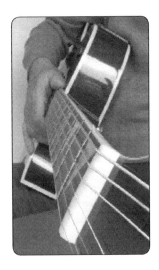

Page 4

2

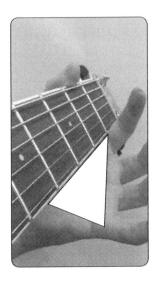

Page 10

FINGER	STRING	FRET
2nd	5th	2nd

3

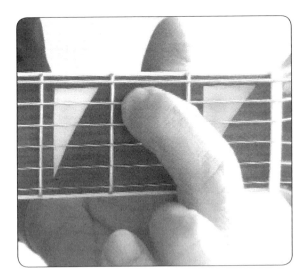

- Thumb not touching 6th string
- Strum 6 strings

E maj7

1

Page 4

2

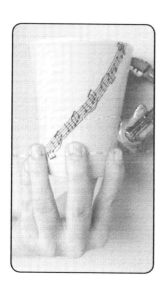

Page 12

FINGER	STRING	FRET
1st	3rd	4th
3rd	5th	6th
4th	4th	6th

3

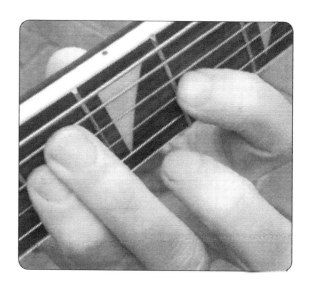

- 1st fingertip in corner of fret
- Strum 6 strings

E7

1

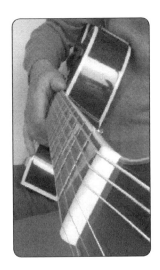

Page 4

2

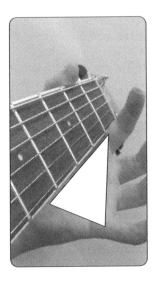

Page 10

FINGER	STRING	FRET
1st	3rd	1st
2nd	5th	2nd

3

- Thumb NOT touching 6th string
- 1st fingertip in corner of fret

E7sus4

1

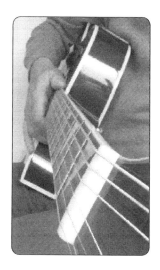

Page 4

FINGER	STRING	FRET
2nd	5th	2nd
3rd	3rd	2nd

3

2

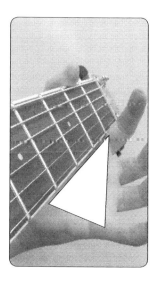

Page 10

- Thumb NOT touching 6th string
- 3rd fingertip in corner of fret

F maj7

1

Page 4

2

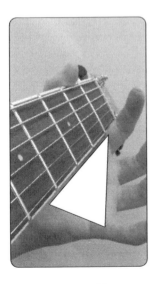

Page 10

FINGER	STRING	FRET
1st	3rd	5th
2nd	2nd	6th

3

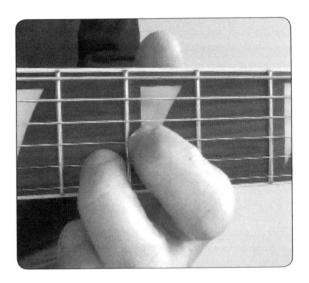

- Thumbcan touch 6th string
- Strum bottom 4 strings

G

1

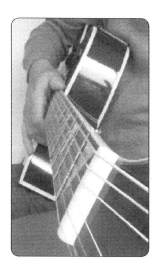

Page 4

2

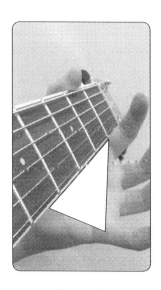

Page 10

FINGER	STRING	FRET
2nd	6th	3rd
1st	1st	2nd

3

- 5th string muted by inside of 2nd finger

G6

1

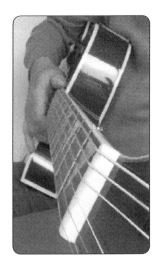

Page 4

2

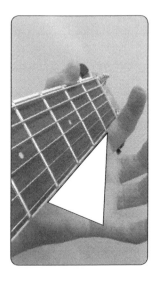

Page 10

FINGER	STRING	FRET
2nd	6th	2rd

3

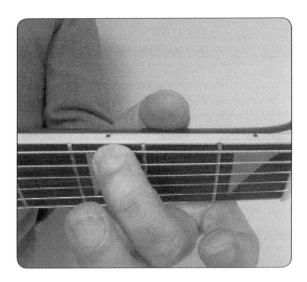

- Mute 5th string with inside of 2nd finger

Gmaj7

1

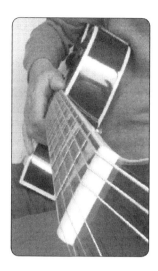

Page 4

2

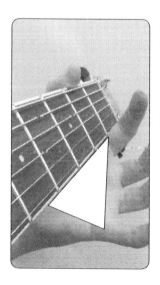

Page 10

FINGER	STRING	FRET
1st	1st	2nd

3

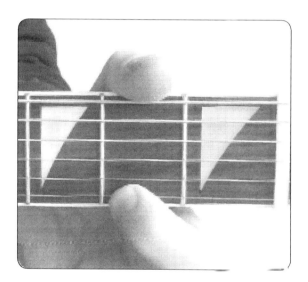

- Thumb can touch 6th string
- Strum bottom 4 strings

MOST PLAYED GUITAR CHORDS

In

Alphabetical Order

A

1

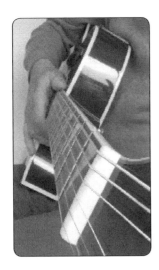

Page 4

2

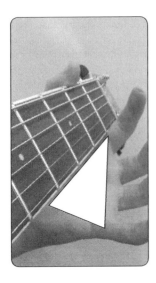

Page 10

FINGER	STRING	FRET
1st	4th	2nd
2nd	3rd	2nd
3rd	2nd	2nd

3

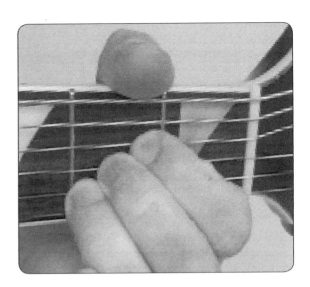

- Thumb touches 6th string
- Squeeze 1st & 2nd fingers together
- This makes room for 3rd finger

A7sus4

1

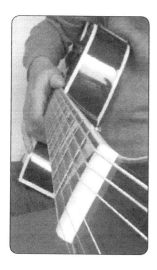

Page 4

2

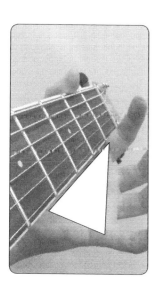

Page 10

FINGER	STRING	FRET
1st	4th	2nd
3rd	2nd	3rd

3

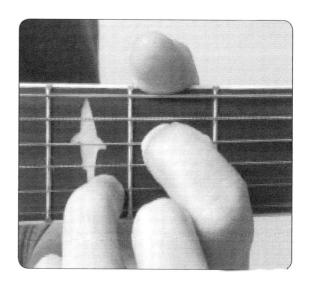

- Thumb touches 6th string
- 1st fingertip in corner of fret
- 3rd fingertip in middle of fret

Amaj7

1

Page 4

2

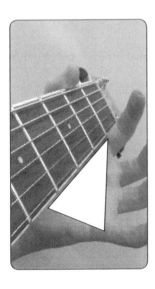

Page 10

FINGER	STRING	FRET
1st	3rd	1st
2nd	4th	2nd
3rd	2nd	2nd

3

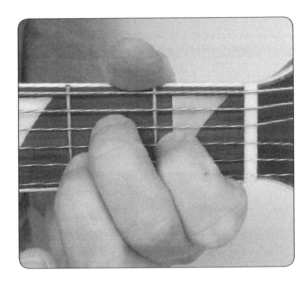

- Thumb touches 6th string
- 1st fingertip in corner of fret
- 2nd fingertip in middle of fret

Bm

1

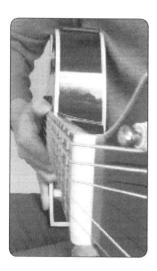

Page 4

2

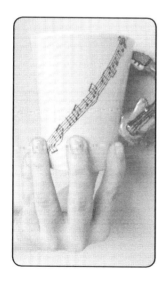

Page 12

FINGER	STRING	FRET
1st	5 strings	2nd
2nd	2nd	3rd
3rd	4th	4th
4th	3rd	4th

3

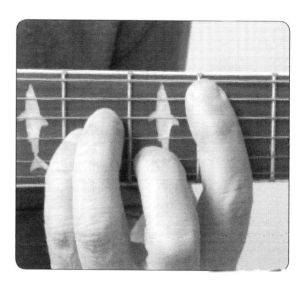

- 1st finger bars 2nd fret
- 1st fingertip touches 6th string
- 3rd fingertip in middle of fret

Bm

An Easier Way

1

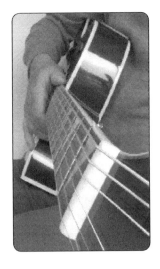

Page 4

2

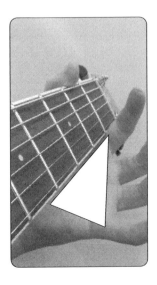

Page 10

FINGER	STRING	FRET
1st	1st	2nd
2nd	2nd	3rd
3rd	3rd	4th

3

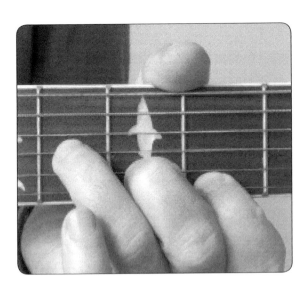

- Thumb touches 6th string
- 1st fingertip in corner of fret
- Strum bottom 4 strings only

B₂

Often played instead of B

1

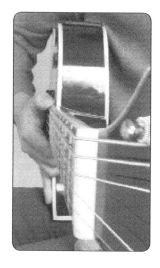

Page 4

2

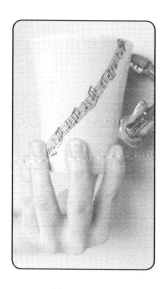

Page 12

FINGER	STRING	FRET
1st	5th	2nd
3rd	4th	4th
4th	3rd	4th

3

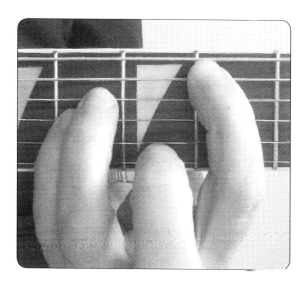

- 1st fingertip touches 6th string
- 2nd finger hovers over 2nd string

B7

1

Page 4

2

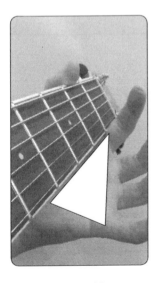

Page 10

FINGER	STRING	FRET
1st	4th	1st
2nd	5th	2nd
3rd	3rd	2nd

3

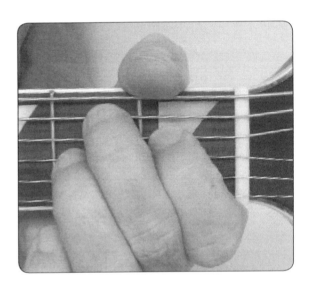

- Thumb touches 6th string
- 1st fingertip in corner of fret
- 2nd fingertip in middle of fret

C

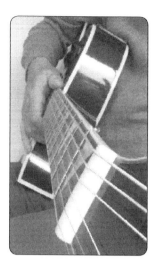

1

Page 4

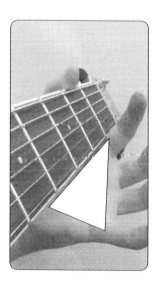

2

Page 10

FINGER	STRING	FRET
1st	2nd	1st
2nd	4th	2nd
3rd	5th	3rd

3

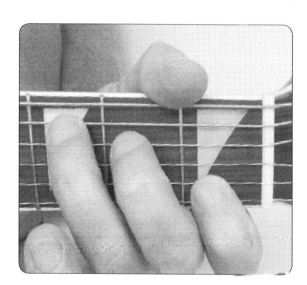

- Thumb touches 6th string
- 1st fingertip in corner of fret
- 3rd fingertip in middle of fret

C7

1

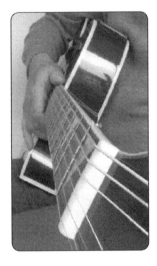

Page 4

2

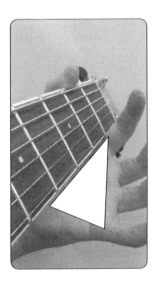

Page 10

FINGER	STRING	FRET
1st	2nd	1st
2nd	4th	2nd
3rd	5th	3rd
4th	3rd	3rd

3

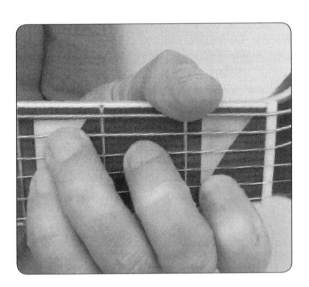

- Thumb touches 6th string
- 1st & 2nd fingertips in corner of frets
- 3rd & 4th fingertips in middle of frets

C#m

1

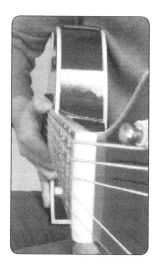

Page 4

2

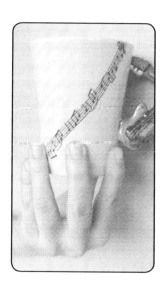

Page 12

FINGER	STRING	FRET
1st	5 strings	4th
2nd	2nd	5th
3rd	4th	6th
4th	3rd	6th

3

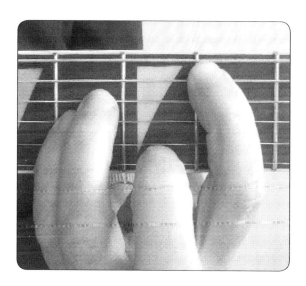

- 1st finger bars across 5 strings
- 1st fingertip touches 6th string

1

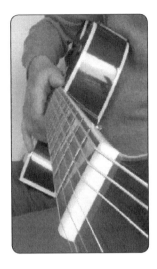

Page 4

2

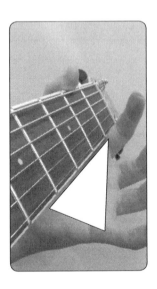

Page 10

D

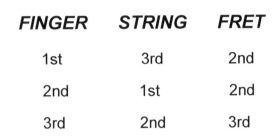

FINGER	STRING	FRET
1st	3rd	2nd
2nd	1st	2nd
3rd	2nd	3rd

3

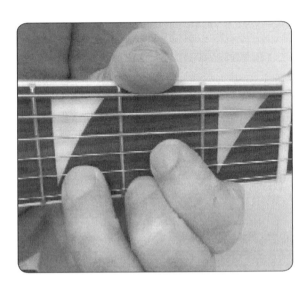

- Thumb touches 6th string
- 1st fingertip in corner of fret
- 3rd fingertip in middle of fret

D/F#

1

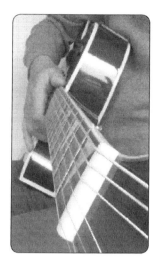

Page 4

2

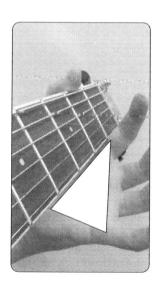

Page 10

FINGER	STRING	FRET
Thumb	6th	2nd
1st	3rd	2nd
2nd	1st	2nd
3rd	2nd	3rd

3

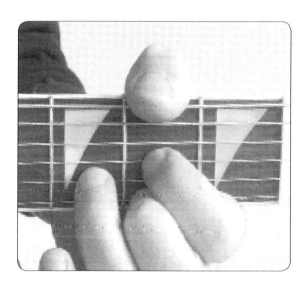

- Thumb plays 6th string 2nd fret
- 1st fingertip in corner of fret
- 3rd fingertip in middle of fret

Dm

1

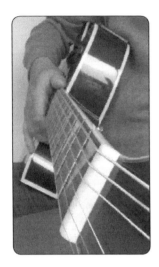

Page 4

2

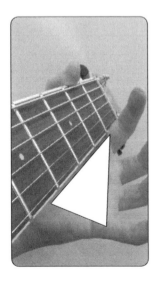

Page 10

FINGER	STRING	FRET
1st	1st	1st
2nd	3rd	2nd
3rd	2nd	3rd

3

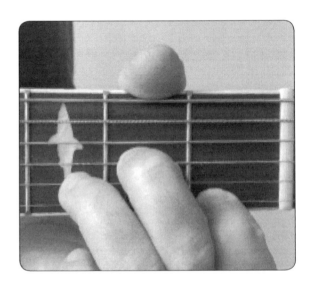

- Thumb touches 6th string
- 1st fingertip in corner of fret
- 3rd fingertip in middle of fret

D7

1

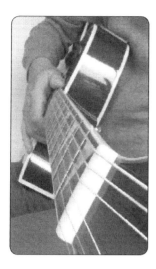

Page 4

2

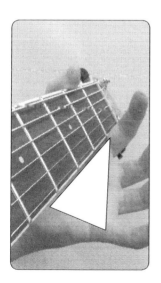

Page 10

FINGER	STRING	FRET
1st	2nd	1st
2nd	3rd	2nd
3rd	1st	2nd

3

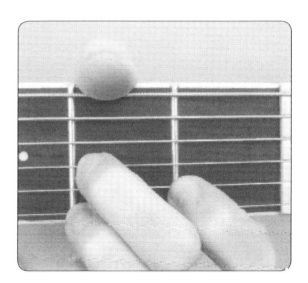

- Thumb touches 6th string
- 1st fingertip in corner of fret
- 2nd fingertip can be in middle of fret

Dm7

1

Page 4

2

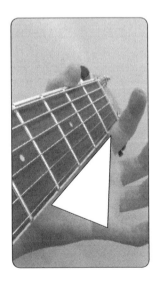

Page 10

FINGER	STRING	FRET
1st	1st	1st
1st	2nd	1st
2nd	3rd	2nd

3

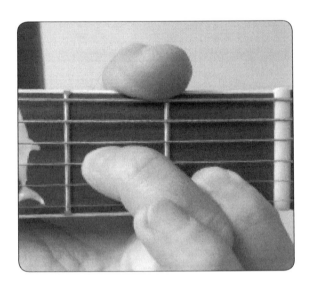

- Thumb touching 6th string
- 1st finger presses 1st and 2nd string
- 1st finger in middle of fret

Dsus4

1

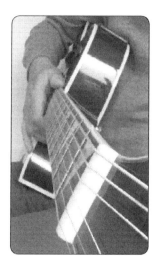

Page 4

2

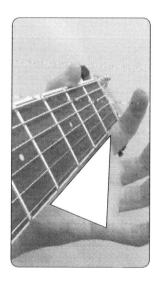

Page 10

FINGER	STRING	FRET
1st	3rd	2nd
3rd	2nd	3rd
4th	1st	3rd

3

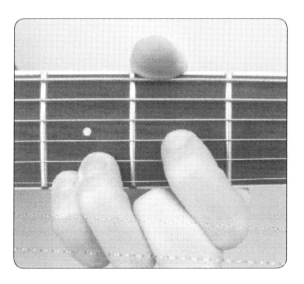

- Thumb touching 6th string
- 1st fingertip in corner of fret
- 3rd fingertip in middle of fret

E

1

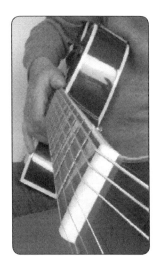

Page 4

2

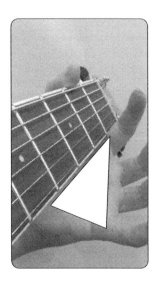

Page 10

FINGER	STRING	FRET
1st	3rd	1st
2nd	5th	2nd
3rd	4th	2nd

3

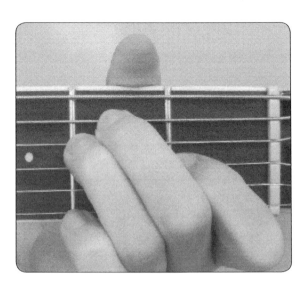

- Thumb NOT touching 6th string
- 1st fingertip in corner of fret

E sus4

1

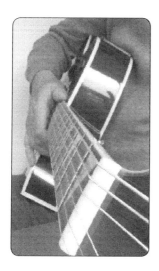

Page 4

2

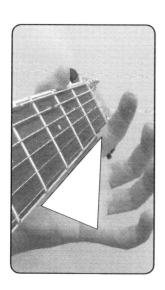

Page 10

FINGER	STRING	FRET
1st	5th	2nd
2nd	4th	2nd
3rd	3rd	2nd

3

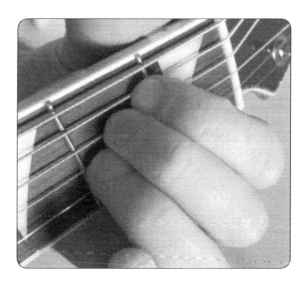

- Thumb not touching 6th string
- Squeeze 1st & 2nd fingers together
- This makes room for 3rd finger

Em7

1

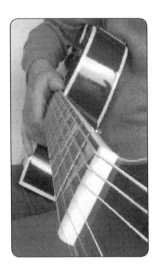

Page 4

FINGER	STRING	FRET
1st	5th	2nd
2nd	4th	2nd
3rd	2nd	3rd
4th	1st	3rd

3

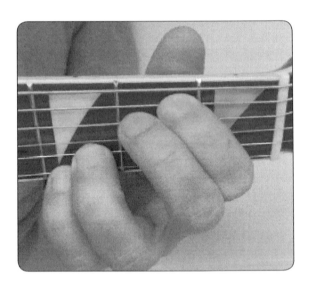

2

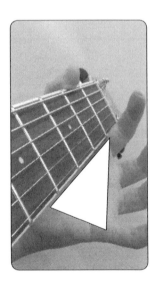

Page 10

- Thumb NOT touching 6th string
- Sometimes the 1st string is played open

Em/G

1

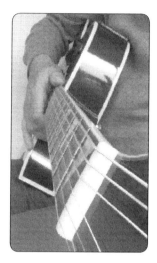

Page 4

2

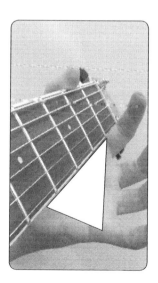

Page 10

FINGER	STRING	FRET
1st	5th	2nd
2nd	4th	2nd
3rd	6th	3nd

3

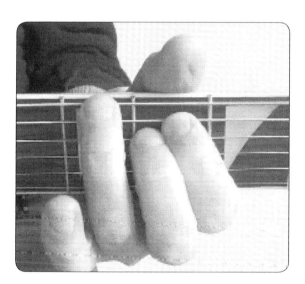

- Thumb NOT touching 6th string
- 3rd fingertip in corner of fret
- Can be played with 1st & 2nd fingers

F

1

GRAB

FINGER	STRING	FRET
1st	1st	1st
1st	2nd	1st
2nd	3rd	2nd
3rd	5th	3rd
4th	4th	3rd

- Grab the guitar neck
- Side of 1st finger pressing strings

F

The Easier Way

1

FINGER	STRING	FRET
1st	2nd	1st
1st	2nd	1st
2nd	3rd	2nd
3rd	4th	3rd

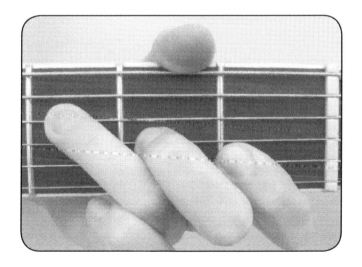

- Hand in at back
- Tumb touching 6th string
- Side of 1st finger pressing strings

FINDING F DIFFICULT?

All chords are played from either the Thumb / Triangle hand position or The Bar Chord hand position. *F is the exception.* It does *not* have a triangle. And it's played with a different thumb position.

TRY THIS

1. Grab the guitar neck first

2. Then move your fingers into position

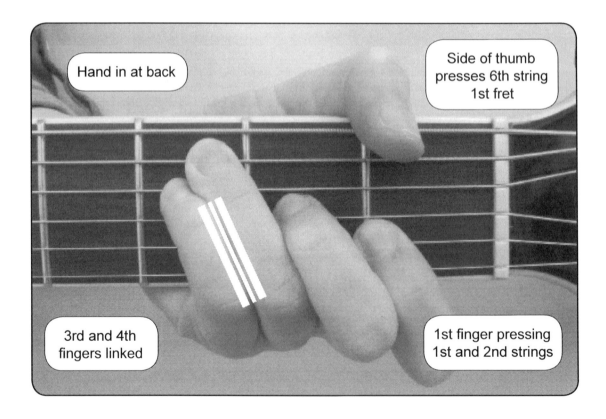

Hand in at back

Side of thumb presses 6th string 1st fret

3rd and 4th fingers linked

1st finger pressing 1st and 2nd strings

Many people spend a lifetime struggling with F. Because it is usually the first chord they need where two strings are pressed by the same finger, many of them *pull the hand out from behind the guitar neck.* **THIS IS FATAL.** The palm of your hand must go ***in and up behind the guitar***.

GRAB YOUR GUITAR

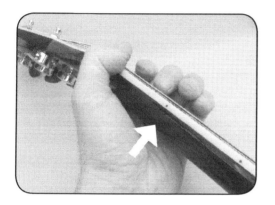 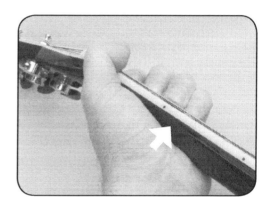

Here I'm changing from G to F. Can you look behind the guitar neck? *My hand is grabbing the guitar.*

And at the same time my fingers are moving into position, with *the thumb rolling sideways.* It presses the 6th string 1st fret for a deeper sound.

Now can you see why F chord change is so difficult to learn? For most peope it has to be practiced *very, very, slowly* at first. Then can you speed it up.

If you can retain a good sound while holding the guitar in one hand *(picture right)* you can play F really well.

The

F

Test

Here is a great way to practice F. It is a slow motion of exactly how professionals do it. Can you do each step very slowly at first? Then you can gradually speed them up until you can do them all in one move.

STEP 1

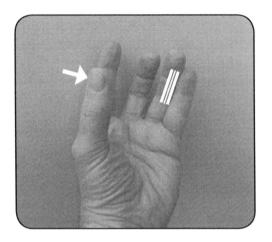

Claw hand and link
3rd and 4th fingers

STEP 2

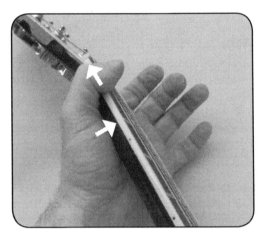

Hand in at the back, with your thumb rolling sideways. This makes it easier for your 1st finger to press two strings.

STEP 3

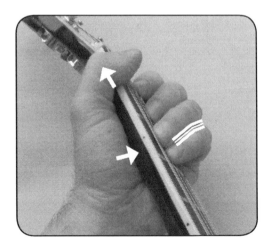

Palm pushing towards
3rd and 4th fingers

Professional guitarists link their 3rd and 4th fingers. It makes four fingers now feel like three.

This gives you more control and improves your sound. Also changing to F becomes faster and easier.

- F is also played as a bar chord

- Lower thumb down behind guitar neck

- Then slide 1st finger up until it is over 6 strings

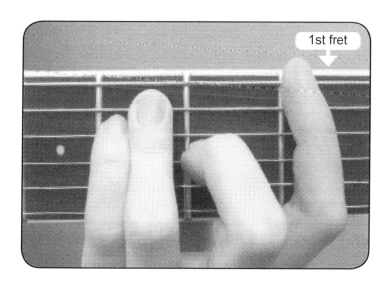

Fmaj7

1

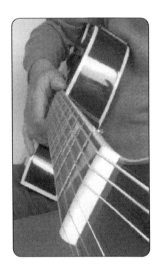

Page 4

2

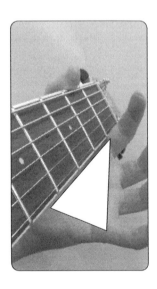

Page 10

FINGER	STRING	FRET
1st	2nd	1st
2nd	3rd	2nd
3rd	4th	3rd

3

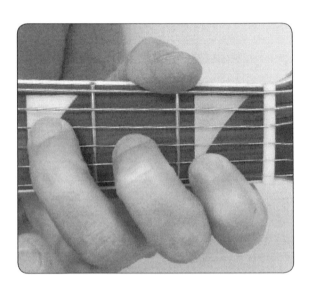

- Thumb touching 6th string
- Fingertips in corner of frets
- 1st string must sound

F#m

1

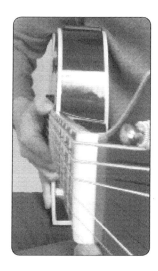

Page 4

2

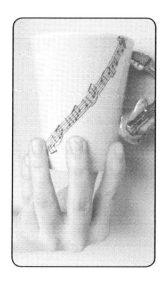

Page 12

FINGER	STRING	FRET
1st	6 strings	2nd
2nd	5th	4th
3rd	4th	4th

3

- 1st finger bars 6 strings on 2nd fret

G

1st way

1

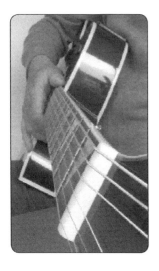

Page 4

2

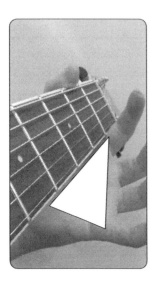

Page 10

FINGER	STRING	FRET
2nd	6th	3rd
3rd	1st	3rd

3

- 1st finger not touching string
- 5th string muted by inside of 2nd finger

G

2nd way

1

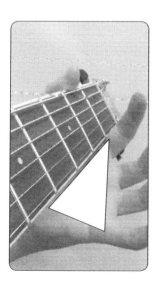

Page 4

2

Page 10

FINGER	STRING	FRET
2nd	6th	3rd
3rd	2nd	3rd
4th	1st	3rd

3

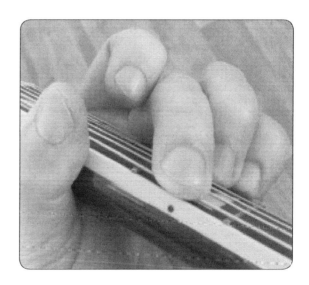

- Thumb can touch 6th string
- 5th string muted by inside of 2nd finger
- Ist finger not hovers over 5th string

G

3rd way

1

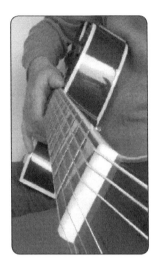

Page 4

2

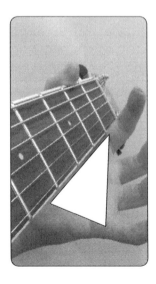

Page 10

FINGER	STRING	FRET
3rd	6th	3rd
4th	1st	3rd

3

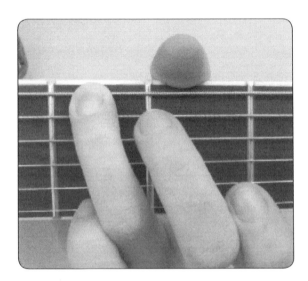

- Thumb can touch 6th string
- 5th string muted by inside of 3rd finger
- 1st & 2nd fingers hover over strings

MORE ABOUT G

Learning G as shown here is one of the key reasons why people give up playing guitar. It may be easier in the short-term. But it leads to many unnecessary obstacles later.

- It never sounds quite right

- It makes changing to C and D quite difficult

- It limits your ability to add bass runs and ornamentation

Do you play G like this? It will help you greatly to simply lift your first finger to mute the 5th string (*shown below*). It will sound much better and you can continue to play it until you have perfected the two more difficult G's on the next page. As well as giving you more musical options, they make chord changing easier too.

YES

- 5th string muted by inside of 2nd finger

- Strum 6 strings (*Only 5 sound*)

- Thumb may or may not touch 6th string (*optional*)

- 1st finger not touching string

WITH THIS G

- Em is mostly played with the 1st and 2nd fingers

- Also you won't have to move your 3rd finger when changing to D, Cadd9 or Em7

- You get a rich sound

YES

WITH THIS G

- Em is mostly played wit the 2nd and 3rd fingers

- 2nd and 3rd fingers move as one unit when changing to C, D and other chords *(Page 134)*.

- It frees up your 1st and 2nd fingers to add bass runs, and ornamentation

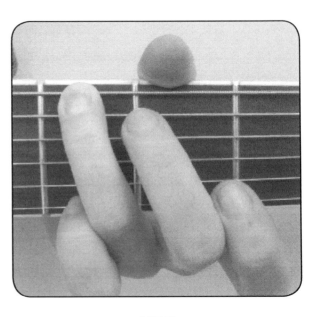

YES

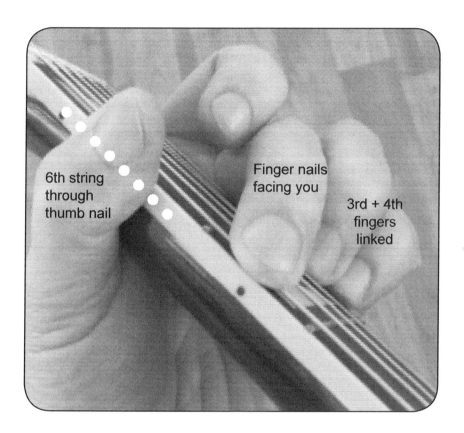

- 5th string muted by side of 2nd finger

- Thumb lightly touching 6th string
  (If your hand is big enough)

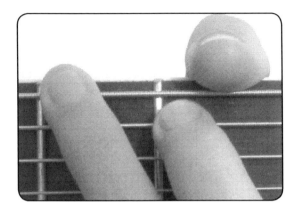

When you strum six strings you should only hear five.

In this picture the 5th string is muted by the inside of the 3rd finger.

The 2nd finger is **not touching** the 5th string.

If their hand is big enough, many of them keep the thumb touching the 6th string, even though it does not impact on sound. It does however, save them moving it on the next chord change often, *(because it's already preset for that chord)*. You may not be able to do this if your hand is small.

G Bar chord

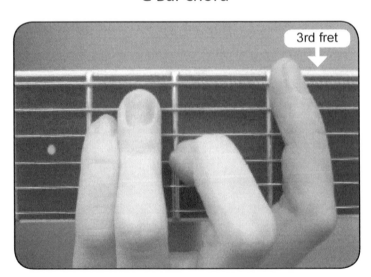

3rd fret

Learning G professionally is more difficult....but it does pay off. Top guitarists play it at least three different ways. This opens up a lifetime of endless possibilities. Here is G as a bar chord.

G sus4

1

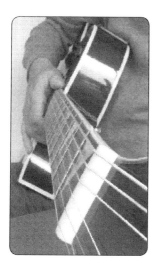

Page 4

2

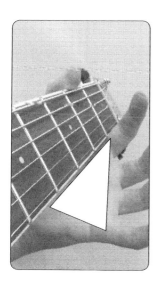

Page 10

FINGER	STRING	FRET
3rd	6th	3rd
4th	1st	3rd
1st	2nd	1st

3

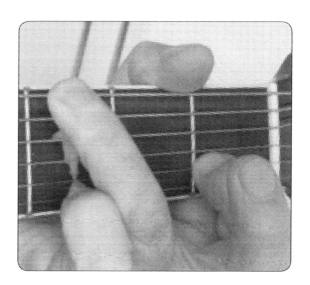

- Thumb can touch 6th string
- 5th string muted by inside of 3rd finger

G7

1

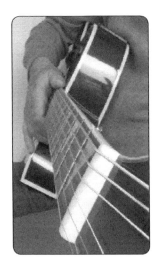

Page 4

2

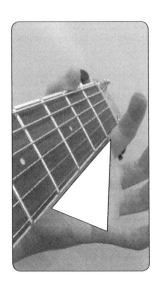

Page 10

FINGER	STRING	FRET
3rd	6th	3rd
1st	1st	1st

3

- 5th string muted by inside of 3rd finger

Gmaj7

1

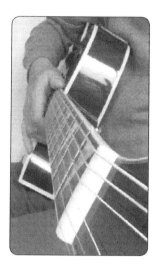

Page 4

2

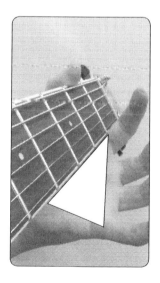

Page 10

FINGER	STRING	FRET
2nd	6th	3rd
1st	1st	2nd

3

- Mute 5th string with inside of 2nd finger

BAR
CHORDS
MADE EASY

BAR CHORDS
MADE EASY

The word bar can be very misleading. Most people interpret it literally and bar their first finger straight. If you look at any top guitarist, you will clearly see that *the first finger is curved and turned out.*

- Hold the book up with this page open

- Hold it with just your thumb and 1st finger

- Put your finger over one of these pictures

- This is the same as barring on a guitar

- Copy the curved finger

- Nail turned out about 30°

NO   YES

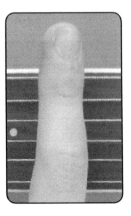 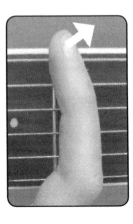

You also need a good thumb and wrist position. It has to be low and fairly centred. Your wrist should be low too.

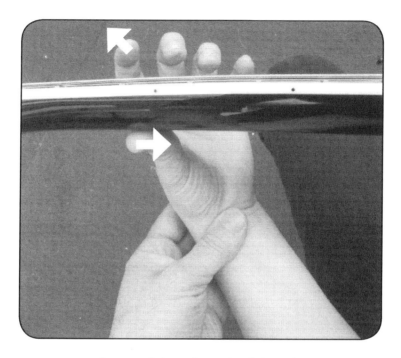

Low wrist and centred thumb

This is not as easy to do as it looks. If you're having difficulty it will help to ask a friend to hold your wrist in position as shown here. After a few minutes, you should start finding it easier to do.

Turning your bar finger out about a 30° angle helps greatly to bring the other fingers out in front of the fretboard and in line with the strings. Now bar chords are much easier to play.

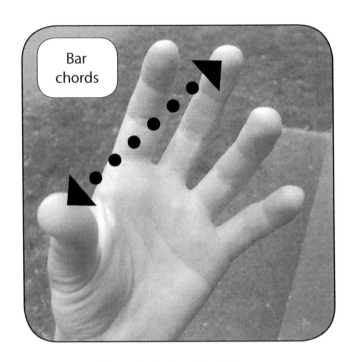

Thumb facing 2nd finger

Bar Chord Test

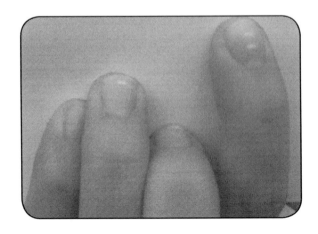

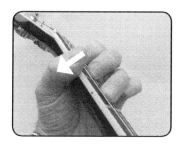

CHANGING TO BAR CHORDS

Finger C chord with thumb on top

Slide your **THUMB ONLY** down at the back. Keeping it centred, slowly *tilt the guitar neck by leaning forward.* Your fingers should be still in the C position.

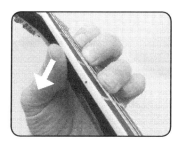

With your hand **CLAWED** move fingers into the Bm shape while in the air

Now drop Bm shape onto the fret-board

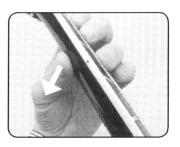

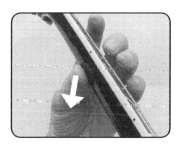

Many top guitarists start sliding the thumb down behind the neck from the second beat of the open chord they are playing. It is fully in position for the bar chord before the fourth beat is played.

During the last upstroke they start moving the fingers in the direction of the bar chord. If you practice this *IN 3 MOVES* as shown here, and with *your fretting hand only,* you should quickly get it.

It's the very same, and gives you complete control over bar and power chords.

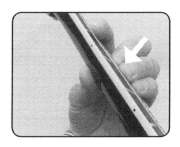

PERFECT
BAR CHORD
HAND POSITION

Handset the same
as holding a mug

To play bar chords on natural ability your **fingers are set parallell** to the frets. Practice this with great care. It should soon become easy and effortless.

FINGERS
PARALLELL

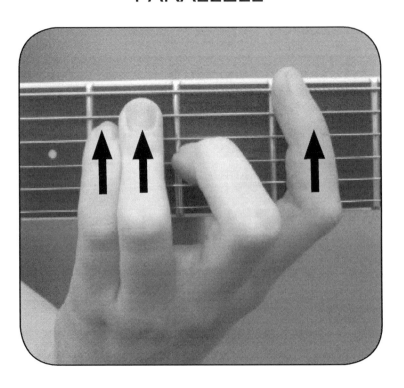

PLAYERS VIEW

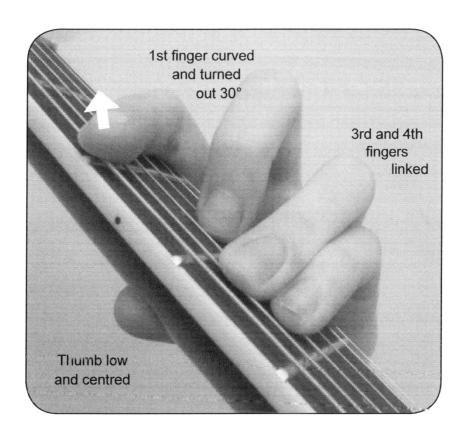

1st finger curved
and turned
out 30°

3rd and 4th
fingers
linked

Thumb low
and centred

- Fingers **narrow** as you slide towards bridge

- Fingers **widen** as you slide towards tuning heads

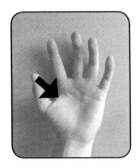

Claw and slide
thumb over

Here is yet another of the great secrets of playing guitar. It's very difficult to move four fingers in different directions at the same time.

Can you claw your hand and link the 3rd and 4th fingers? Your hand now feels as if it has only three fingers.

This is easier to control especially when you're changing chords.

Thumb now facing
2nd finger

Link 3rd +
4th fingers

Playing guitar is much easier when you make

- *4 fingers feel like 3*

- *3 feel like 2 and*

- *2 feel like 1*

It's done by always looking for opportunities to link your fingers. You can even practice bar chord shapes without a guitar if you claw first (pictured right).

4 fingers
feel like 3

A SIMPLE TIP

1. Hold a mug in your fretting

2. Claw your hand and link 3rd & 4th fingers

3. Smae feeling as playing a bar chord

4. Holding your shape, take the mug away

5. Place your fingers on the fretboard

6. This is your hand position for bar chords

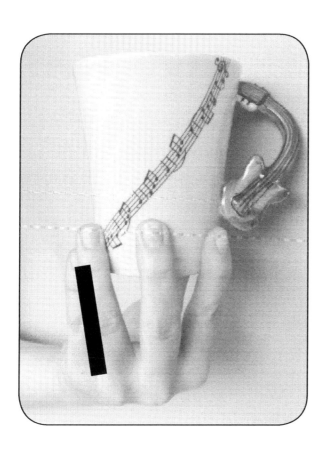

100 CHORDS
IN 3 STEPS

If you learn just eight notes on the 6th string *(Step 1)*, and 6 E chord positions *(Step 2)* you will have over 100 new bar chords *(Step 3)*.

STEP 1

Open 6th String	E	**#** = Up one fret	
		(Towards soundhole)	
1st fret	F	Example	
3rd fret	G	G = 3rd fret	
		G#= 4th fret	
5th fret	A		
7th fret	B		
		b = Down one fret	
8th fret	C	(Towards tuning heads)	
		Example	
10th fret	D	B = 7th fret	
12th fret	E	Bb= 6th fret	

Bar chords are much easier to learn if you know the most played E and A shaped chords. It's wiser to learn the E shapes completely before moving on.

STEP 2

Copy

E chord

→

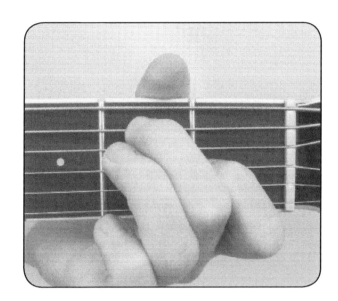

And

Lift 1st finger and strum 6 strings	→	Em
Strum 3 strings of Em. The 6th 5th and 4th	→	E5
Move 3rd finger to 3rd string 2nd fret	→	E7sus4
Take off the 3rd finger	→	Em7
Add 1st finger to 3rd string 1st fret	→	E7

STEP 3

FROM

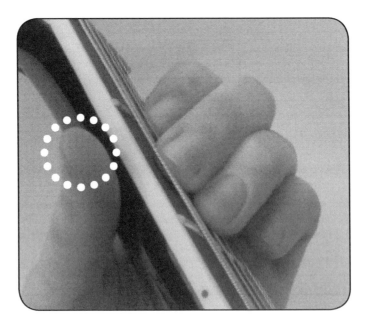

Take off all 3 fingers

Now do the E chord again with 2nd 3rd and 4th fingers
as shown on top of the next page.

TO

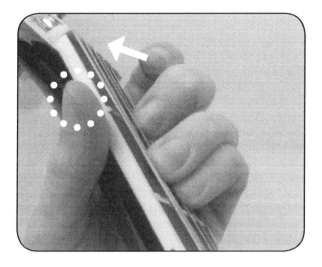

Now lower your thumb and at the very same time, add your 1st finger across and outside the nut

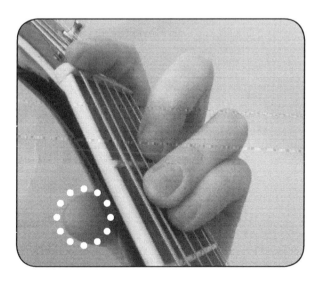

The reason this sounds good is because the nut is sounding the 6th 2nd and 1st strings. If it wasn't there, you would have to curve your first finger across the nut as shown here.

Then lift the 1st finger as shown here and you have an Em. This is usually one of the easiest chords to learn on guitar. Without the nut, this is the only way it can be played.

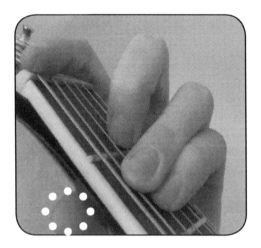

FROM

From this Em can you move your 4th finger down one string? This is E7sus4

If you put your 2nd finger back on and take off the 4th finger you now have E7

And if you put your 4th finger on the 4th string we're back to E where we started

TO

If you move up one fret and repeat the chord sequence you get F, Fm, F7sus4, F7 and back to F. The note your first finger presses on the 6th string is F. This helps to give you the name of the chords.

And it is why I asked you, at the start of this lesson, to learn them off by heart. This, combined with the finger changes, make it a 7 or m7 or 7sus4 and many more.

The 3rd fret would give you all the G bar chord shapes because your 1st finger is playing G note on the 6th string. The 4th fret gives you the G# bar chords. When your first finger bars across six strings on the 7th fret you have the B bar chords.

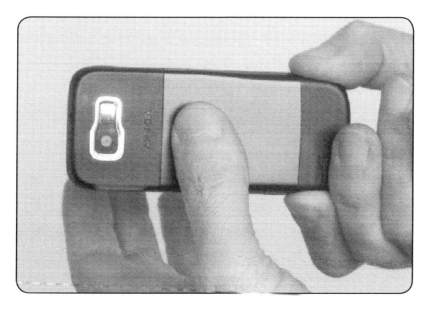

You can practice on your phone or "The Paper Guitar" *(Page 38)*

If you're having difficulty, with any of these moves, it's highly likely that your thumb has moved out of position behind the neck. To succeed with bar chords

You must start with and maintain a good thumb position

PLAYERS VIEW

- Your fingers **_narrow_** in as you slide towards sound hole

- Your fingers **_widen_** as your hand slides towards tuning pegs

1st finger curved

Nail turned out 30°

Thumb and fingertips

CLAWED

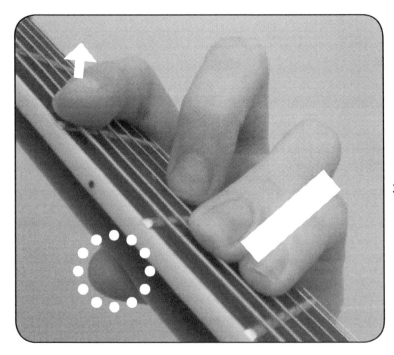

3rd and 4th
fingers
linked

THUMB

Centred and low

Five skills top guitarists share

1. Thumb centred and low

2. 1st Finger curved out slightly

3. Thumb and fingertips clawed

4. 3rd and 4th fingers linked together

5. Fingers narrow in and widen out as you move up and down the fretboard

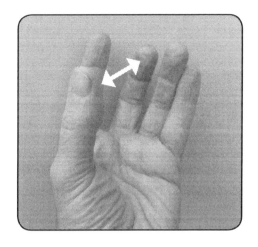

Professionals do all these skills at the same time. If you practice them individually you will soon find it much easier to play bar chords.

Pushing your thumb against the 1st finger helps greatly to improve sound

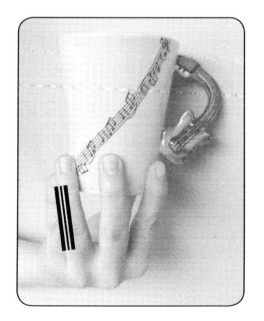

Your hand should feel as if you are holding a mug full of water. While holding it as shown here, link your 3rd and 4th fingers.

Then remove the mug and you are left with a perfect hand for bar chords. Hold this hand shape as you approach the guitar neck from underneath.

THUMB

Hold this book up in front of you

Place your thumb over one of these thumbs

One is right.....One is wrong

Can you see how similar this is to holding a real guitar?

Many people play bar chords from a poor thumb position

YES

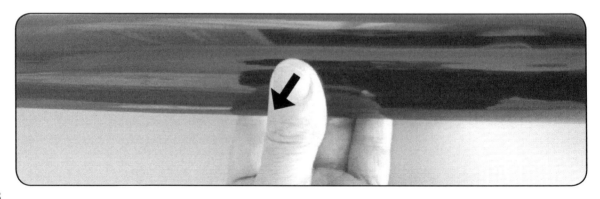

TEST

- Your thumb has a huge impact on how your hand and fingers play guitar.

- Many people leave it behind (picture below) when they try to play. This can be fatal. To play bar chords, your thumb and hand must move up and down the neck as one unit.

- This controls your fingers. And they now go to the corner of the frets without reach or stretch.

NO

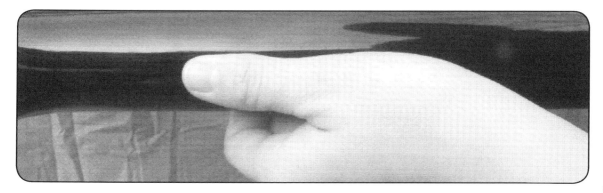

200 CHORDS
IN 3 STEPS

Top guitarists also play A shaped bar chords. With E shaped bar chords only, you'll be constantly going up and down the guitar neck. However, by combining E and A shapes, many chord sequences can be played between three frets.

If you have followed the three steps to learning the E shaped chords, all you have to do is follow the same approach here. This gives you over 200 more chords to choose from.

STEP 1

Open 5th string	A
2nd fret	B
3rd fret	C
5th fret	D
7th fret	E
8th fret	F
10th fret	G
12th fret	A

Can you learn these notes on the 5th string off by heart? This makes it much easier to find A shaped bar chords.

Your hand must approach the guitar from underneath

= Up one fret
(Towards soundhole)

Example

G = 3rd fret

G#= 4th fret

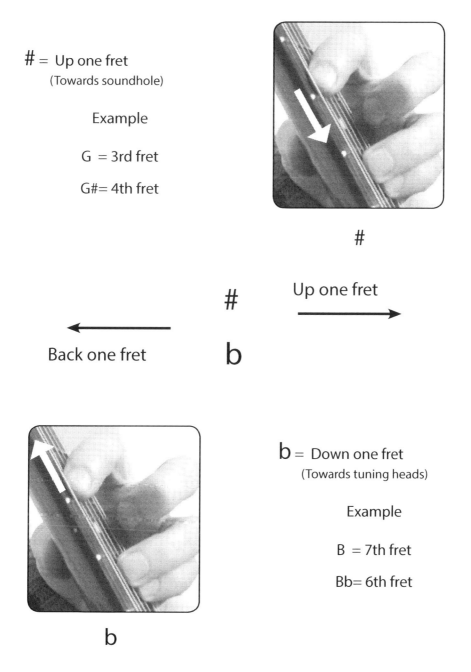

#

Up one fret →

← Back one fret   **b**

b = Down one fret
(Towards tuning heads)

Example

B = 7th fret

Bb= 6th fret

b

Even though A# and Bb give the impression that they are two different chords, they're both the same (barred across the 6th fret)

A SHAPED BAR CHORDS

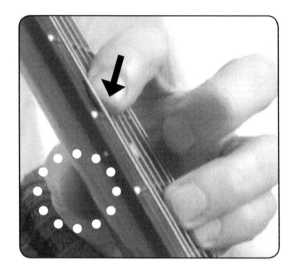

Good guitarists *do not bar across six strings* for these. They bar across five and mute the 6th string with the fingertip.

For open chords (except E's) the 6th string is muted with the thumb.

But because your thumb is now low and centred it cannot mute the 6th string. Instead it is done with the 1st fingertip.

1st fingertip mutes 6th string

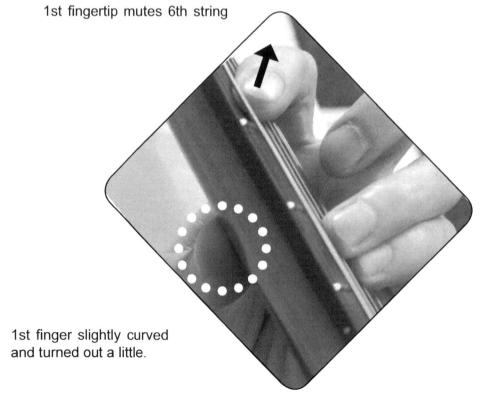

1st finger slightly curved and turned out a little.

STEP 2

A

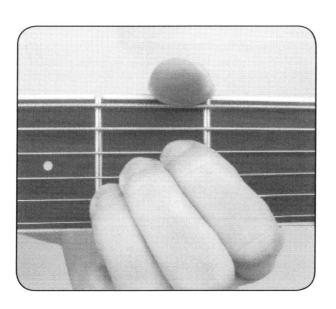

Pull 1st finger to 3rd string 1st fret and move 2nd finger up one string	⟶	Amaj7
From Amaj7 take off 1st finger	⟶	A7
Move 3rd finger up one string	⟶	Asus2
Add 1st finger to 2nd string 1st fret	⟶	Am
Take off 1st finger	⟶	Am7

FROM   TO

From Here   Now do Am again butvwith
Take off all 3 fingers   2nd 3rd and 4th fingers this
                             time

Then lower your thumb and at the very same time,
add your 1st finger across and outside the nut as
shown above right.

The reason this sounds good is because the nut is
sounding the 5th and 1st strings. If it wasn't there,
you would have to curve your 1st finger across the
nut as shown here.

STEP 3

Once you know the A shapes and the notes on the 5th string you are ready for step 3

- The only difference is that you are one string lower with Am

- Turn your fingers around the same as you did with E

- Then curve the 1st finger just outside the nut

Can you see how Am would have to be a bar chord if the nut was not there? From here slide up two frets. This gives you Bm. Up one more fret for Cm. For C#m you would bar on the 4th fret. It's just like how we learned E shaped bar chords. The note on the fret your 1st finger bars, combined with the A shape you are playing, gives you the name of the bar chord.

Top guitarists do not bar six strings for A shaped bar chords. The first fingertip lightly touches and mutes the 6th string (*Page 178*). The 7th fret is the exception. As these are all E type chords, an open 6th string (E) complements them.

CAN YOU DO THIS?

Most top guitarists have what looks like a double jointed 3rd finger. It means they can play A shaped bar chords with the 1st and 3rd fingers only (pictured below).

- With three fingers you quickly run out of space as you move up the guitar neck.

- With a double jointed 3rd finger you can keep moving this very important chord shape up the fretboard.

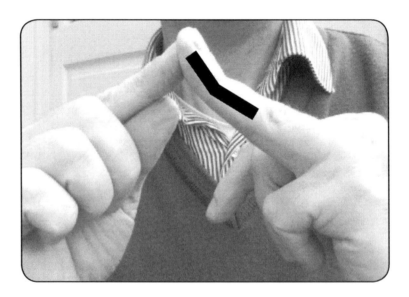

Bend it back

Nobody is born with this skill - *but it can be developed*.

- Bend your 3rd finger back (fretting hand) as shown here a few times every day

- After a few weeks you should be able to start playing A shaped bar chords with it

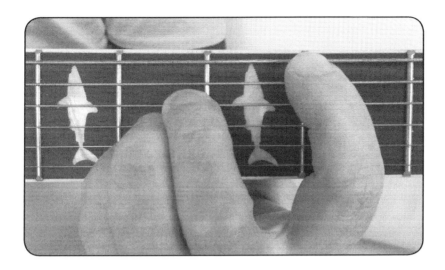

NO

Trying to play bar chords, with a bar finger and the other three fingers in one fret, closes doors. As well as being quite difficult to quickly change into, you run out of space for your fingers once you move past the third fret.

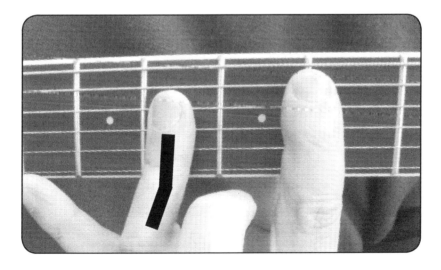

YES

CHORD INDEX

In Alphabetical Order

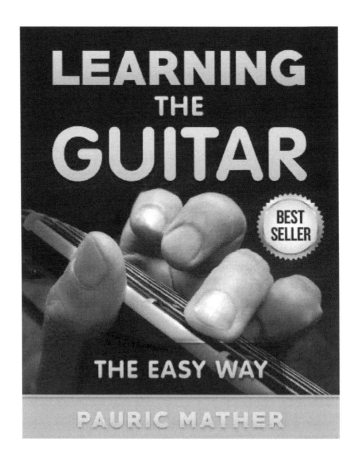

Available in
all major bookstores
and online retailers worldwide